Breastfeeding your baby with a dairy allergy

I have been a pediatric nurse for over ten years. Even with my medical education and background, nothing could prepare me for being a mom. When I saw blood in my baby's stool, I was terrified. When we went to the pediatrician, they reassured me that the blood in the stool is usually caused by a dairy allergy. I was breastfeeding, and evidently my son was allergic to the cow's milk I was consuming. The pediatrician told me if I cut out dairy from my diet, the blood should go away, rest assured, babies usually outgrow this allergy. No dairy? I had just avoided soft cheese for nine months while pregnant, along with all of my other favorites (dirty martinis!). How hard could it be? My mom intuition kicked in, and I wanted to breastfeed. I was not going to eat dairy. I was a strong-willed woman who has to do this for my child…. That lasted about a week. No dairy is hard! I had to come up with meals I could enjoy and would fulfill my normal eating habits, such as Friday night pizza and chocolate chip cookies.

All these questions were running through my head: What exactly is dairy? Can I eat eggs? Is almond milk safe? I knew the obvious choices of milk, cheese, and yogurt, but that was the extent. Therefore, I talked to a nutritionist, and she gave me some advice on what not to eat. Whey and casein are by-products of dairy. I had to look at the ingredient list and omit these. Many lactose-free options include dairy by-products. When the label says lactose-free, it does not mean it is dairy-free. After I talked with the nutritionist, I remember thinking: I can't eat anything. Grocery shopping took twice as long because I had to sit there and read through all the ingredients. This was not conducive to having a baby with me. I had to get shopping done on the breastfeeding/ nap/ only-have-a-few-hours-to-do-anything baby cycle. I wanted to know what I could eat, as well as what I could not eat.

The stress and emotional ride a newborn bestows on a mom takes up most of our thinking time. I already gave birth to half my brain; I could not think about what I was going to eat as well. I pondered whether or not to add basic recipes to this cookbook. Then I remembered how I felt as a new mom, overwhelmed. Some of the recipes in here might seem straightforward, but to help you figure out what you are able to eat once you decide to go dairy-free, I wanted to make it as simple as possible and take out the guesswork. If taking a shower seems like too much work right now, at least you know you can still have a yogurt parfait to start off your morning right!

Hopefully my cookbook eases your stress and provides support to eat dairy-free while you continue to breastfeed. The intent of this recipe book is not only to provide you with tasty recipes, but to give you options! I am not a chef. I am not a doctor. These recipes improved my quality of life, and I hope they can help you. Cooking is my hobby, and I really enjoy making good food. I am a mom of two boys, both of whom had dairy allergies. This cookbook provides you with delicious dairy-free recipes. Enjoy what you eat! Learn more at **www.dairyfreebreastfeedingmama.com.**

Disclaimer: Any action you take upon the information in this book is strictly at your own risk, and I am not liable for any losses or damages. It is the reader's responsibility to check food labels and ingredients for items that may contain dairy.

Acknowledgements

Cooking, blogging, and creating a cookbook with two little ones running around requires a lot of collaboration. I want to express my sincere gratitude to those who contributed to *Dairy-Free Recipes*.

To my mom and dad, I cannot thank you enough for passing on your love for cooking and entertaining. It's hard to put into words how appreciative I am that you were able to spend endless hours with my kids and helping me with my recipes.

I am grateful to my two sisters, Julie Moore and Sarah Rajcic. Thank you to Carissa Winters, Megan Wright, Patty Dodge, Kristin Marino, and all of my friends for your support while developing this book and guiding me along the way.

To my husband and children, thank you for your patience, taste testing, and eating cold dinners due to picture-taking and time spent tweaking ingredients. Drew, since the first conversation about writing a book, you encouraged me to do what I love and I am honored to write this book from our experiences together.

To my angels, the incredible women in my family that cooked for my parents and grandparents, I know you were in the kitchen with me and my mom. Your recipes and love for family will continue to inspire me.

Photographs by Lindsay Izzio

Copyright pending

Table of Contents
Breakfast

- 13 Banana Bread
- 15 Vanilla Chia Seed Pudding
- 16 Toast with Avocado and Eggs
- 17 Toast with Peanut Butter and Banana
- 19 Oatmeal
- 21 Yogurt Parfait
- 22 Strawberry Banana Smoothie
- 23 Baked Pancakes with Fruit Topping
- 25 Corned Beef Sweet Potato Hash

Table of Contents
Pizza

27 Prosciutto Arugula Pizza

29 Pizza with Smoked Chicken Sausage, Brussel Sprouts, and Honey Sweet Potatoes

31 Cauliflower Pizza Crust with Pesto, Tomatoes, and Artichokes

33 BBQ Chicken Pizza

Table of Contents
Side Dishes

- 35 Potato Salad
- 37 Fruit Salsa
- 38 Hummus
- 39 Baked Beans
- 41 Mediterranean Zucchini
- 43 Grandma Betty's Stuffing
- 45 Vegetable Pesto Pasta Salad
- 46 Reney's Tomato Salsa

Table of Contents
Soup

49 Potato Leak Soup

51 Beef Stew

53 Escarole and Beans with Sausage

55 Chicken Artichoke Soup with Quinoa

56 Italian Wedding Soup

57 Grandma Irene's Manhattan Clam Chowder Soup

Table of Contents
Entrees

- 59 Lindsay's Chicken
- 61 Reuben Sandwich
- 62 Meatballs
- 63 Meatloaf Muffins
- 65 Chicken Marsala
- 67 Rotisserie Chicken Salad
- 69 Fish with Tomatoes and Olives
- 71 Slow Cooker Chicken Fajitas

Table of Contents
Entrees

- 73 Spicy Sausage and Broccoli Pasta
- 75 Shrimp Rolls
- 77 Salmon Cakes
- 79 Kielbasa with Potatoes, Bacon, and Pineapple
- 81 Apple Cider Pork Chops
- 82 Chicken Primavera
- 83 Grilled Chicken with Cornell Marinade

Table of Contents
Entrees

85 Sweet Chili Eggplant on Garlic Hummus Toast

87 Fish Tacos

89 Seafood Fra Diavolo

91 Grilled Mushrooms

93 Clam Bake Packets

Table of Contents
Dessert

- 95 Chocolate Chip Cookies
- 97 Maple Coconut Cookies
- 99 Wacky Chocolate Cake
- 100 Carrot Cake
- 101 Cream Cheese Frosting
- 103 Chocolate Covered Bananas with Peanut Butter
- 105 Apple Crisp

Breakfast

Banana Bread

Makes 2 loaves

Instructions

Position the rack in the center of the oven and preheat to 350 degrees F.

Grease 2 loaf pans with non-butter cooking spray. In a large bowl, cream the sugar and shortening. Add eggs and bananas and mix together until combined. In a separate bowl, sift together flour, salt, and baking soda. Add dry ingredients to wet ingredients and mix together.

Divide between the two prepared loaf pans. Bake until the bread is golden brown and a toothpick inserted into the center comes out clean, about 1 hour. Transfer the pans to wire racks and let cool for 5 minutes. Then remove the loaves from the pans and let cool on the racks for at least 10 minutes before serving.

Ingredients

2 cups sugar

1 cup shortening

4 eggs

6 ripe bananas

2 ½ cups flour

1 teaspoon salt

1 teaspoon baking soda

Vanilla Chia Seed Pudding

Serves 4

Instructions

In a medium size bowl, using a fork, mix almond milk, chia seeds, and vanilla extract. Cover and let sit overnight. The next day, scoop mixture into a bowl. Drizzle maple syrup on top, and add strawberries and almonds.

Notes

My inspiration for this recipe comes from my brother-in-law. He is talented in creating healthy, nutritious, and delicious meals. Chia seeds are an excellent source of omega-3 fatty acids, antioxidants, iron, fiber, and calcium. Enjoy this recipe as a dessert or breakfast!

Ingredients

2 cups vanilla almond milk

½ cup chia seeds

½ teaspoon vanilla extract

maple syrup for drizzling

1 cup strawberries, sliced

4 tablespoons sliced almonds (1 tablespoon per serving)

Toast with Avocado and Eggs

Serves 1

Instructions

Toast the bread. In a bowl, whisk the eggs and add salt, pepper, and a splash of water. In a small sauté pan, cook the eggs on medium-low heat, until cooked to your preference.

While the eggs are cooking, cut the avocado in half and remove pit. Smear one half of the avocado on one slice of toast and the other half on the other slice of toast. Place the scrambled, cooked eggs on top of the avocado. Sprinkle sunflower seeds over the scrambled egg. Drizzle with olive oil. Salt and pepper to taste.

Ingredients

2 slices sourdough bread

2 eggs

salt and pepper

1 avocado

1 tablespoon sunflower seeds

olive oil for drizzling

Toast with Peanut Butter and Banana

Serves 1

Instructions

Toast the bread.

While the bread is still warm, spread peanut butter on both slices of toast. Place sliced pieces of banana on peanut butter. Drizzle with honey and enjoy while warm.

Ingredients

2 slices sourdough bread

2 tablespoons peanut butter

1 banana, sliced

honey for drizzling

Oatmeal

Serves 1

Instructions

Warm oatmeal as directed on package. Combine ingredients and enjoy warm. Simple and satisfying!

Notes

I enjoy the comfort of warm oatmeal in the winter. This quick, yummy breakfast will keep your belly full. Use an instant oatmeal of your choice. Do not use a creamy oatmeal. Check the ingredient list for dairy.

Ingredients

1 package instant oatmeal

¼ cup blueberries

¼ cup strawberries, sliced

1 tablespoon candied walnuts

Yogurt Parfait

Serves 1

Instructions

Mix yogurt in a bowl with fruit: blueberries, raspberries, and mango. Top with granola.

Notes

Yogurt parfaits are a healthy, easy breakfast to make. Choose a dairy-free yogurt of your choice.   To make a parfait, pick fruits you like or what is in season. I use fresh fruits, not frozen. Use granola you prefer. Just check the label for dairy products.

Ingredients

1 cup vanilla dairy-free yogurt

¼ cup blueberries

¼ cup raspberries

¼ cup mango, diced

½ cup granola

Strawberry Banana Smoothie

Serves 2

Instructions

Combine orange juice, strawberries, banana, and yogurt in a blender until smooth. Pour into a glass and enjoy.

Notes

Freeze several ripe bananas by peeling them and placing in sealable plastic bag. Freeze for up to 2 weeks. For strawberries, frozen purchased strawberries are the easiest option.

Ingredients

½ cup orange juice

1 cup frozen strawberries

1 frozen ripe banana

1 cup soy or almond vanilla yogurt

Baked Pancakes with Fruit Topping

Serves 4-6

Instructions

Preheat oven to 400 degrees F.

Whisk together eggs, soy milk, salt, sugar, and vanilla extract. In a separate bowl, whisk together flour and baking powder. Add the dry ingredients into the wet ingredients. Whisk together. Let the mixture sit for 10 minutes.

Heat an 8 inch cast iron skillet in the oven with the vegan butter. Pour the batter into the cast iron pan carefully. Bake until the pancake is golden brown and puffed up (about 15 minutes).

While the batter cooks, make the berry syrup. Heat the berries in a small saucepan with the maple syrup. Heat until the mixture thickens (you should still be able to see the berries).

Cut the pancake into wedges and serve the warm berry syrup on top. Dust with powdered sugar.

Notes

This is a perfect weekend breakfast the entire family will like!

Ingredients

3 eggs

1 cup vanilla soy milk

½ teaspoon salt

¼ cup sugar

1 teaspoon vanilla extract

1 ½ cups flour

1 tablespoon baking powder

2 tablespoons vegan butter

1 bag (1 pound) frozen mixed berries

⅓ cup maple syrup

powdered sugar

Corned Beef Sweet Potato Hash

Serves 4-6

Instructions

Rinse corned beef brisket. Place in crock pot and sprinkle seasoning packet over brisket. Add beer and enough water to cover most of the brisket. Cook on high for 6-8 hours or low for 10-12. Once cooked, let crockpot cool and place brisket in the refrigerator.

The next day after corned beef is done cooking, preheat oven to 400 degrees F. On a large baking sheet lined with parchment paper, spread the sweet potatoes, yellow pepper, red pepper, and onion in a single layer. Drizzle with olive oil, salt, and pepper. Bake for 30 minutes, turning once halfway through.

In a cast iron skillet, heat 2 tablespoons of olive oil on medium-high heat. Add garlic and cook until fragrant, about 1 minute. Careful not to burn the garlic. Add roasted vegetables, corned beef, and smoked paprika. Mix together softly. Cook until desired crispiness and heated through. Flip occasionally, but do not overmix to prevent mushing the sweet potatoes. I suggest serving with a side of eggs!

Notes

I love St. Patrick's Day. I make corned beef and cabbage every year. I buy the biggest brisket in order to make an extra meal with leftovers. My two recipes for corned beef leftovers: corned beef sweet potato hash and a really tasty Reuben sandwich (on page 61).

The brisket for the hash should be cooked the day before or overnight. If you would like, you can also cut and roast the vegetables the day before and put it all together in the morning.

Ingredients

Corned Beef Ingredients

corned beef brisket with seasoning packet

12 ounce dark beer

water

Hash Ingredients

2 large sweet potatoes, peeled and diced

1 yellow pepper, seeded and diced

1 red pepper, seeded and diced

1 medium sized yellow onion, diced

olive oil

salt and pepper

2 cloves garlic, chopped

3 cups corned beef, diced

1 teaspoon smoked paprika

Pizza

Prosciutto Arugula Pizza

Serves 4

Instructions

Preheat oven according to pizza dough instructions.

Hand shape or roll pizza dough to desired shape, about ¼ inch thickness. Place on a large, greased baking sheet or pizza pan, pressing out any air bubbles, forming enough dough to fit the pan.

In a small bowl, combine olive oil, oregano, garlic, and sprinkle of salt and pepper. Spread mixture over pizza dough. Then spread dairy-free ricotta over dough. Bake dough according to the package's instructions or until desired crispiness, about 15-20 minutes.

While the dough is cooking, in a large bowl, add arugula, lemon juice, salt, and pepper. Drizzle with olive oil. Toss gently and set aside.

Once pizza crust is done cooking, place on cutting board. Top pizza crust with prosciutto pieces, then arugula salad. Enjoy!

Notes

I made this pizza with cheese before eating dairy-free and loved it. I removed the cheese to make a dairy-free version and it came out just as good! When choosing a pizza dough, make the dough as thin as you can make it. This pizza tastes better as a thin crust, not thick and doughy, like a flatbread. Check pizza dough for dairy.

Ingredients

1 bag (16 ounces) purchased uncooked pizza dough

3 tablespoons olive oil

¼ teaspoon oregano

2 garlic cloves, grated

salt and pepper

½ cup dairy-free ricotta

4 cups baby arugula

juice of ½ lemon

olive oil for drizzling

2 ounces prosciutto (approximately 3 slices), pulled apart into pieces

Pizza with Smoked Chicken Sausage, Brussels Sprouts, and Honey Sweet Potatoes

Serves 4

Instructions

Preheat oven to pizza dough instructions.

Hand shape or roll pizza dough to desired shape, about ¼ inch thickness. Place on a large, greased baking sheet or pizza pan, pressing out any air bubbles, forming enough dough to fit pan.

In a large skillet on medium heat, add chicken sausage. Fry until crispy, about 10 minutes.

Meanwhile, in a large bowl, mix Brussels Sprouts and olive oil, with a sprinkle of salt and pepper. Add Brussels Sprouts mix to frying pan. Continue cooking for about 3-4 minutes, stirring continuously. You want the Brussels Sprouts to soften and brown, but not burn. Once done, shut heat off and set the pan aside.

In the large bowl, mix the sweet potato ribbons and honey and set aside.

Add the garlic to the melted vegan butter with a sprinkle of salt and pepper. Spread garlic butter all over pizza dough. Then in a single layer, place sweet potato and honey mixture over pizza dough. Top with cooked Brussels Sprouts and chicken sausage mixture. Place in oven on the center rack. Cook per dough instructions or to desired crust crispiness, approximately 15 minutes. Grab a fork and enjoy!

Ingredients

1 bag (16 ounces) purchased uncooked garlic and herb pizza dough (white pizza dough tastes good too!)

1 package (12 ounces) smoked andouille chicken sausage, sliced into ¼ slice pieces

1 bag (10 ounces) shaved Brussels Sprouts

¼ cup olive oil

salt and pepper

1 bag (6 ounces) sweet potato ribbons

¼ cup honey

3 cloves garlic, minced

2 tablespoons vegan butter, melted

Cauliflower Pizza Crust with Pesto, Tomatoes, and Artichokes

Serves 2-4

Instructions

Preheat oven to cauliflower pizza crust instructions.

To prepare the pesto, in a food processor, pulse basil and pine-nuts together. Add garlic and pulse again. Add olive oil and a sprinkle of salt and pepper, and pulse until smooth.

Cook cauliflower crust according to package's instructions. After crust cooks, top with layer of pesto, tomatoes, and artichokes. Set oven to broil and place pizza back in hot oven for 5 minutes, just enough to warm toppings. Keep an eye on the pizza and make sure it doesn't overcook.

Notes

This pizza is super healthy and dairy-free, of course. When cooking with pesto, make it yourself or find dairy-free pesto. Most pesto from a jar has cheese in it.

Ingredients

Pesto Ingredients

2 cups basil

⅓ cup pine-nuts (can substitute with walnuts if needed)

2 cloves garlic

¼ cup olive oil

salt and pepper

Pizza Ingredients

1 box (11 ounces) purchased frozen cauliflower pizza crust

pesto

1 large beefsteak tomato, diced

½ cup marinated artichokes, drained (add more if desired)

BBQ Chicken Pizza

Serves 4

Instructions

Preheat oven to pizza dough instructions.

Hand shape or roll pizza dough to desired shape, about ¼ inch thickness. Place on a large, greased baking sheet or pizza pan, pressing out any air bubbles; forming enough dough to fit pan.

Heat a tablespoon of oil in a frying pan on medium heat. Add onion and sauté for 5 minutes until soft and lightly browned. Add spinach, some salt and pepper, and cook for two minutes, stirring frequently. Remove from heat.

Spread desired amount of pizza sauce on the pizza dough. Use a spoon to spread the spinach and onion mixture. Careful, it will be hot! Spread chicken. Drizzle BBQ sauce over entire pizza pie. Cook per instructions on the pizza dough package, approximately 15 minutes.

Notes

This is the first pizza I made to satisfy my desire for pizza after starting a dairy-free diet. My husband was surprised at how good it was without cheese on it! Add toppings to make it how you like it. I suggest bacon or hot banana peppers!

To make life easier, for the chicken, I get a BBQ flavored rotisserie chicken and pull it apart. For the sauce, pick out a jar of pizza sauce without any cheese in it. When buying the dough, double check for dairy.

Ingredients

1 bag (16 ounces) purchased uncooked pizza dough

1 tablespoon olive oil

1 medium onion, diced

1 bag (6 ounces) spinach

salt and pepper

1 jar pizza sauce

2 cups cooked chicken, chopped

BBQ sauce for drizzling

Side Dishes

Potato Salad

Makes 20 servings

Instructions

In a large pot, place the potatoes into cold, salted water. Bring water to a boil and cook until tender but still firm.

Carefully, drain the potatoes when done and place them into a mixing bowl. Roughly slice them or cut in quarters, if preferred. Sprinkle still-hot potatoes with vinegar, olive oil, salt and pepper. Add the celery, cucumbers, mayonnaise, and mustard; toss gently to combine. Add quartered eggs and parsley and toss again. Cool to room temperature, cover, and refrigerate overnight. Before serving, add more mayonnaise, salt, and pepper, if needed.

Notes

This potato salad is a perfect potluck BBQ side dish! Prepare the day before, because it has to sit overnight.

Ingredients

4 pounds boiling potatoes, peeled

½ cup white wine vinegar

½ cups olive oil

1 teaspoon salt

¼ teaspoon black pepper

1 cup celery, chopped

3 cucumbers, peeled and chopped

2 cups mayonnaise

5 tablespoons Dijon mustard

20 hard boiled eggs, peeled and quartered and cooled

1 cup parsley, chopped

Fruit Salsa

Serves 4

Instructions

For the chips: preheat oven to 350 F.

Combine sugar and cinnamon in a small bowl. Spray the tops of the tortillas with cooking spray and sprinkle with the cinnamon sugar. Cut each tortilla into 10 wedges. Spread on a cookie sheet in a single layer. Bake about 8-10 minutes, until crispy. Remove from oven and let cool.

To make the salsa: combine the apples, pear, and lime juice in a medium bowl. In the microwave, warm peach preserve for 10 seconds to soften and add to apple and pear mixture. Mix together. Gently fold in the strawberries and blueberries. Cover and chill in the refrigerator for one hour.

To serve, assemble chips around bowl of chilled fruit salsa.

Ingredients

Chips Instructions

3 tablespoons sugar

½ teaspoon cinnamon

5 10-inch flour tortillas

olive oil based cooking spray

Fruit Salsa Instructions

2 apples, diced

1 pear, diced

juice of 1 lime

3 tablespoons peach preserve

8 ounces strawberries, diced

4 ounces blueberries, halved

Hummus

Makes 2 cups

Instructions

Place chickpeas in a food processor with the tahini and garlic. Puree. Add juice of all three lemons and process for 10 seconds. Add salt, cumin, and olive oil. Process for another 20 seconds or until creamy. Serve with crackers or pita bread.

Ingredients

1 can (20 oz) chickpeas, drained

⅔ cup tahini

2 cloves garlic

3 lemons

½ teaspoon salt

1 teaspoon cumin

2 tablespoons olive oil

Baked Beans

Serves 6-8

Instructions

Preheat oven to 325 degrees F.

On the stove, put a heavy-bottomed pot over medium heat. Add bacon and cook until bacon begins to crisp, about 8-10 minutes. Add onion and cook until the onion is softened, about 5 more minutes. Stir in ketchup, tomato puree, brown sugar, vinegar, Worcestershire sauce, salt and pepper, and cayenne. Mix together well. Bring to a simmer and cook for 5 minutes. Stir in the beans, mix and cover. Carefully, place pot into oven and bake for 1 hour. After 1 hour, remove lid and continue baking until the sauce thickens and beans begin to brown, about 15 minutes. Remove from oven and allow to cool slightly before serving. Serve warm or at room temperature.

Ingredients

8 slices of bacon, chopped

1 medium onion, chopped

¾ cup ketchup

¾ cup tomato puree

½ cup firmly packed dark brown sugar

¼ cup cider vinegar

1 tablespoon Worcestershire sauce

salt and pepper to taste

¼ teaspoon cayenne pepper

2 cans (28 ounce) red beans, drained and rinsed

Mediterranean Zucchini

Serves 4

Instructions

Using a veggetti slicer, veggetti zucchini into a bowl (or buy prepackaged zucchini veggetti if you do not have a veggetti slicer). In a large sauté pan on medium heat, heat 2 tablespoons of the oil from the sun-dried tomato jar. Add zucchini noodles. Cook, stirring occasionally, for 5 minutes. Pour cooked zucchini noodles back into the bowl. Keep warm.

In the sauté pan, on medium-low heat, add 1 tablespoon of sun-dried tomato oil and 4 tablespoons of sun-dried tomatoes. Add garlic and cook for 1-2 minutes. Add spinach and wine and continue cooking until spinach is wilted. Remove sauté pan from heat. Add zucchini noodles back to the pan, with walnuts and mix all together. Salt and pepper to taste. Transfer everything to a bowl and serve.

Ingredients

2 zucchinis

3 tablespoons sundried tomato oil from the jar, plus 4 tablespoons sundried tomatoes from the jar, sliced

3 gloves garlic, chopped

2 cups spinach

½ cup dry white wine

¼ cup chopped walnuts

salt and pepper

Grandma Betty's Stuffing

Serves 6-8

Instructions

Preheat oven to 350 degrees F. Prepare 9x13 baking pan with non-dairy cooking spray.

In a large sauté pan, on medium heat, sauté sausage until crisp. Break up into pieces as it cooks, approximately 10 minutes. Remove sausage from pan, leaving the fat in the pan. In the same pan with the sausage fat, sauté onions and celery until onions become soft and translucent, approximately 5 minutes.

In a large bowl, add stuffing and pour melted vegan butter. Add apples, then cooked sausage, onions, and celery. Mix together. Pour apple juice over mixture and fold together.

Pour stuffing into 9x13 prepared pan and bake until warmed through, about 45 minutes. Remove earlier if you like your stuffing soft

Ingredients

1 bulk (no casing) pork breakfast sausage (1 pound)

¾ cup onion, chopped

1 ½ cups celery, chopped

12 cups herbed stuffing bread

2 sticks vegan butter, melted

4 cups sweet apples, peeled and chopped (Approximately 5 small apples, such as Macintosh or Empire)

4 cups apple juice

If using plain stuffing bread, you can add these spices for more flavor:

½ teaspoon pepper

1 tablespoon dried sage

1 teaspoon poultry seasoning

Vegetable Pesto Pasta Salad

Serves 6

Instructions

Preheat oven to 425 degrees F.

Place aluminum foil on 2 sheet pans and spray with cooking spray. In a small bowl, mix balsamic vinegar, mustard, garlic, herbs de Provence, salt, and 2 tablespoons of olive oil. Whisk together. In a large bowl, add cut vegetables and toss with the dressing. Spread vegetables on the sheet pans in a single layer. Roast for 20-30 minutes, flipping half way through. While the vegetables roast, bring a large pot of salted water to a boil and cook the pasta per the directions on the package. Reserve ¼ cup pasta water before draining.

To make the pesto see page 31

Combine the cooked pasta, pesto, and beans. Slowly add reserved pasta water as needed to coat. Add roasted vegetables and combine. Top with a drizzle of balsamic. Serve warm or cold.

Notes

Vegetable pesto pasta salad is healthy and delicious! This dish is tossed with tasty balsamic roasted vegetables and fresh dairy-free pesto pasta! Eat it cold or hot for a flavorful addition to your next meal!

Ingredients

Vegetable Ingredients

olive oil cooking spray

1 tablespoon balsamic vinegar

1 teaspoon mustard

2 garlic cloves, finely chopped

1 teaspoon dried herbs de Provence or Italian herbs

1 teaspoon salt

2 tablespoons olive oil

2 cups broccoli florets

8 ounces sliced mushrooms

1 red bell pepper, seeded and cut into 1 inch pieces

1 zucchini, cut into ¼ inch thick rounds

1 yellow squash, cut into ¼ inch thick rounds

1 pint cherry tomatoes, halved

Pasta Ingredients

basil pesto (dairy-free recipe on page 31)

½ pound spiral pasta

1 can (15-ounce) cannellini beans, drained and rinsed

balsamic vinegar for drizzling

Reney's Tomato Salsa

Makes 4 cups

Instructions

In a large bowl, add the diced tomatoes and diced green pepper. In a food processor, fitted with a steel blade, add half of the diced tomatoes and green peppers. Then add the rest of the ingredients except the crushed tomatoes. Process for 5 seconds, creating a vegetable mash. Add the vegetable mash back to the bowl with the remaining diced tomatoes and diced green pepper.

Add the crushed tomatoes and mix well. Cover the salsa and chill in the refrigerator for at least 1 hour. Serve with a side of tortilla chips.

Notes

Every summer when the tomatoes are fresh, my mom makes this amazing salsa! This salsa is incredibly fresh and flavorful! As an added bonus, it is healthy!

When using the food processor, do not over-process the vegetables; it will become soupy! If you prefer less heat, only use 1 jalapeno.

Ingredients

2 large tomatoes, diced

1 green pepper, seeded and diced

1 yellow onion, chopped

1 tablespoon fresh cilantro, minced

1-2 jalapeno peppers, seeded and chopped (depending on how spicy you prefer)

2 teaspoons lime juice

1 teaspoon ground cumin

1 teaspoon dried oregano

1 teaspoon Red Hot sauce

¼ teaspoon black pepper

¼ teaspoon salt

¼ teaspoon red pepper flakes

¼ teaspoon cayenne pepper

2 cups canned crushed tomatoes

Soup

Potato Leak Soup

Serves 4-6

Instructions

To clean the leaks: cut off the tough dark green tops and roots and discard. Cut into ¼ inch slices. Rinse well under water using a colander (leaks are dirty).

Melt vegan butter on medium-low heat in a pot. Add chopped leaks, stir, cover, and cook until leaks are softened (about 10 minutes). Do not brown the leaks. Add diced potatoes, broth, bay leaf, thyme, salt and pepper. (When adding the thyme, roll between fingers before tossing into the pot to release the flavor.) Increase the heat and bring to a simmer. Once simmering, lower heat and simmer for 20 minutes until potatoes are softened through. Remove and discard bay leaf. Using an immersion blender or standing blender, blend soup until smooth. Be careful not to burn yourself; it will be hot. Add parsley and serve with bacon if desired.

Notes

Not in the mood to clean leaks? Use a bag of frozen leaks already cleaned and sliced! Just defrost and discard excess water before cooking.

Ingredients

3 large leeks, approximately 3 cups after chopping

2 tablespoons vegan butter

2 pounds yellow potatoes, peeled and diced (approximately 6 medium size potatoes)

4 cups chicken broth

1 bay leaf

½ teaspoon dried thyme

1 teaspoon salt

¼ teaspoon pepper

¼ cup chopped parsley (optional)

crumbled bacon (optional)

Beef Stew

Serves 4

Instructions

Preheat oven to 350 degrees F.

In a Dutch oven, on medium–high heat, add olive oil and beef. Brown beef on all sides. Shut off heat. Have beef broth ready to pour. Dust beef with flour and mix for a few seconds. Add beef broth and turn the heat back to medium. Add onions, garlic powder, thyme, bay leaf, and bring to a boil. Once boiling, carefully place Dutch oven in oven and cook for 1 hour, covered . After an hour, add carrots and potatoes. Cover and cook in the oven for another hour. Discard thyme sprigs and bay leaf.

Ingredients

2 tablespoons olive oil

1 pound boneless beef stew meat (such as beef chuck or bottom round) cut into 1-inch cubes

1 tablespoon flour

1 quart (32 ounces) beef broth

1 cup onions, chopped

1 teaspoon garlic powder

4 fresh thyme sprigs

1 bay leaf

6 carrots, chopped

3 medium yellow potatoes, peeled and cut into 1 inch pieces

Escarole and Beans with Sausage

Serves 4

Instructions

In a large pot or Dutch oven, squeeze the sausage out of the casing. On medium heat, cook sausage for about 10-15 minutes until cooked through, breaking into small chunks with a wooden spoon as it cooks. Add chopped garlic and sauté for 1 minute. Stir to make sure garlic does not burn. The garlic should become fragrant. If you can't smell it, keep cooking another minute. Add the can of cannellini beans with the juices from the can. Do not rinse the beans. Add the bag of escarole, chicken broth, salt, and pepper. Cover and cook for 20 minutes. Mix every once in a while. Serve and enjoy warm.

Ingredients

1 pound spicy Italian sausage links

3 garlic cloves, chopped

1 can (15 ounces) cannellini beans

1 bag (15 ounces) fresh chopped escarole

1 quart (32 ounces) chicken broth

½ teaspoon pepper

¼ teaspoon salt

Chicken Artichoke Soup with Quinoa

Serves 6-8

Instructions

In a slow cooker on high, add chicken, marinated artichokes, artichokes, and cannelloni beans, and cook for 3 hours. After 3 hours, add lemon juice, spinach, salt, and pepper, and cook for an additional hour. Add cooked quinoa, and mix through. Salt and pepper to taste.

Notes

Cook quinoa a head of time according to package instructions. Quinoa needs to be rinsed before cooking. I cook my quinoa in chicken stock instead of water to give it extra flavor!

Ingredients

4 pounds boneless, skinless chicken thighs

1 jar (12 ounces) marinated artichokes

1 can (13 ounces) artichokes

1 can (15 ounces) cannelloni beans with the juices

juice of 2 lemons

1 bag (6 ounces) spinach

¼ teaspoon salt

¼ teaspoon pepper

2 cups cooked quinoa

Italian Wedding Soup

Serves 6-8

Instructions

In a big stock pot, on medium heat, warm olive oil. Add carrots, celery, and onions. Sauté for about 8- 10 minutes until soft.

To the pot of vegetables, add white wine and stir through for about a minute. Add chicken broth and bring to a boil. Add pasta and reduce to a simmer, cooking for 8 minutes. Add dill and meatballs to the pot and simmer for a two more minutes. Add spinach and cook for another minute. Add salt and pepper to taste.
Serve and enjoy!

Ingredients

2 tablespoon olive oil

2 carrots (approximately 1 cup) cut into ¼ inch pieces

2 celery stalks (approximately 1 cup) cut into ¼ inch pieces

1 small yellow onion (approximately 1 cup) chopped

½ cup dry white wine

8 cups chicken broth

1 cup small pasta, such as ditalini or tubettini pasta

¼ cup dill, minced

20-25 meatballs (recipe on page 62)

6 ounces (4 cups) baby spinach

Grandma Irene's Manhattan Clam Chowder Soup

Serves 4-6

Instructions

In a large stock pot, over medium heat, cook bacon until crispy. Add onion, celery, garlic, and red pepper, and cook, covered, stirring occasionally. Cook until soft, approximately 8-10 minutes. Stir in the tomato paste. Mix through the vegetables. Add clam juice, thyme, bay leaf, potatoes, and carrots. Bring to a boil then reduce to a simmer and cover. Cook until potatoes are soft, about 10 minutes. Add tomatoes, squeezing each tomato into pieces as you add them. Add the juices from the can. Add minced clams. Cover and bring to a simmer. Once simmering, remove from heat. Salt and pepper to taste and serve with a nice toasted loaf of bread!

Notes

One of my dad's favorite, and often asked for dinners, is his mother's tasty Manhattan Clam Chowder soup. I hope you enjoy a modified version of my Grandmother's soup!

Ingredients

3 slices bacon, diced

1 large yellow onion (approximately 2 cups) chopped

2 celery stalks, chopped

5 cloves garlic, minced

pinch of red pepper

¼ cup tomato paste

5 cups clam juice

3 thyme sprigs

1 bay leaf

2 white potatoes, cubed (approximately 1 pound)

2 carrots (approximately 1 cup) diced

1 can (28 ounces) whole, peeled tomatoes, with juices

1 ½ cups minced clams, drained (4 cans of 6.5 ounces)

Entrees

Lindsay's Chicken

Serves 4

Instructions

Preheat oven to 400 degrees F.

Salt and pepper the chicken. Dredge the chicken in flour. To a sauté pan, on medium heat, add olive oil and 1 tablespoon vegan butter. Then add the chicken to the pan. Cook chicken until it has a nice crisp, about 5 minutes per side for thighs. (This might be shorter if using a thin sliced chicken.) Once done, place chicken in a glass 7x11 baking dish. Set aside. Using the same frying pan, turn the heat to low and add wine. Using a wooden spoon, stir, scraping the little bits of chicken off the bottom of the pan. Add whole jar of marinated artichokes, including the marinade juices. Add lemon juice, one tablespoon of vegan butter, capers, and chicken broth. Simmer for 5 minutes. Pour sauce over chicken. Bake 400 degrees for 30 minutes or until internal temperature of the chicken is 165 degrees F. Serve alone or over pasta.

Notes

I live in Rochester, NY, where chicken French is on almost every menu. Chicken French is a delicious lemon-butter chicken dish. I combined ingredients from two of my favorite chicken dishes: Chicken French and Chicken Piccata. I call my creation Lindsay's chicken! I have made this recipe with chicken tenders and chicken breasts thinly sliced. The amount of time you cook the chicken will be altered depending on the type of chicken you decide to use.

Ingredients

4-5 chicken cutlets (such as boneless, skinless chicken thighs)

salt and pepper

1 cup flour

3 tablespoons olive oil

2 tablespoons vegan butter, separated (optional)

½ cup dry white wine

1 jar (12 ounces) marinated artichokes

juice of ½ lemon

¼ cup capers, drained

½ cup chicken broth

Reuben Sandwich

Makes one sandwich

Instructions

Mix together ingredients for Thousand Island dressing in a small bowl and set aside.

Spread vegan butter on one side of the sliced bread. On the other side, smear your Thousand Island dressing generously. In a frying pan, place the bread, butter side down. To the same pan, plop a scoop of sauerkraut and desired amount of corned beef slices. Cook the corned beef and sauerkraut to heat through. Grill the bread to your preference. Place the meat and sauerkraut on the grilled bread and make into a sandwich.

Notes

My first job was working in a cafe. My passion for cooking grew as I watched the owner cook. He taught me the trick to making a Reuben sandwich is using a fresh loaf of bread and warming all the ingredients in the pan. If you prefer not to cook the corned beef brisket, you can use deli meat corned beef. Store bought Thousand Island dressing usually does not contain dairy. The recipe for cooking corned beef in a slow cooker is on page, 25.

Ingredients

Thousand Island dressing Ingredients

½ cup mayonnaise

¼ cup ketchup

¼ cup dill relish

salt and pepper

Sandwich Ingredients

vegan butter

2 slices sliced rye bread or bread of your choice

Thousand Island dressing (recipe above)

1 can (14 ounces) sauerkraut, drained

corned beef, sliced (recipe for homemade corned beef on page 25)

Meatballs

Makes 30-35 meatballs

Instructions

Preheat oven to 350 degrees F.

In a large bowl, add all ingredients. Mix together until all ingredients have been evenly mixed throughout. Meatballs are mixed best using your hands! To shape the meatballs, use a spoon to roll meatballs into 1 –1 ½ inch balls and drop onto a baking sheet lined with parchment paper. Bake for 30 minutes until cooked through to internal temperature of 165 degrees F and slightly browned.

Note

We eat meatballs weekly in my house. We eat them with spaghetti, on meatball sandwiches or in my Italian wedding soup recipe! If you would like to freeze meatballs, place chilled meatballs in freezer safe plastic bags, label, and freeze for up to two months.

Ingredients

1 pound ground beef

1 pound ground sweet Italian sausage, casing removed

2 teaspoons garlic powder

¼ large yellow onion, grated (approximately 2 tablespoons)

¼ cup parsley

2 eggs

1 cup plain white bread crumbs (not Italian seasoned. Those have dairy in them)

salt and pepper

Meatloaf Muffins

Serves 6

Instructions

Preheat oven to 350 degrees F.

Spray 6-muffin tin cup pan with a non-butter cooking spray. Add breadcrumbs to a large bowl. Using a cheese grater, grate onion over bread crumbs. Mix until all breadcrumbs are wet. Mix in beef, egg, garlic power, tomato ketchup, thyme, beef bouillon, and pepper. Dividing evenly among the 6 cups, press mixture down firmly into the muffin tin cups.

Combine glaze ingredients in a small bowl. Spoon glaze over top of meatloaf muffins. Bake for 30-35 minutes, until internal temperature is 160 degrees F. Let stand for 15 minutes before serving.

Note

To make fresh bread crumbs, place 2 slices of dairy-free soft white sliced bread in a food processor. With the steel blades, pulse until crumbled. Check beef bouillon or beef powder ingredients for dairy.

Ingredients

Meatloaf Ingredients

olive oil cooking spray

½ cup plain, unseasoned breadcrumbs

½ red onion

1 pound ground beef

1 egg

1 teaspoon garlic powder

¼ cup tomato ketchup

1 teaspoon dried thyme

1 beef bouillon cube, crumbled or 1 teaspoon beef powder

¼ teaspoon black pepper

Glaze Ingredients

¼ cup ketchup

1 tablespoon cider vinegar

½ tablespoon brown sugar

Chicken Marsala

Serves 6

Instructions

Sprinkle salt and pepper over chicken. In a large skillet, on medium heat, heat 1 tablespoon of olive oil. Add the chicken and cook until golden brown on both sides, approximately 8-10 minutes. Chicken may not be cooked through as it will continue to cook in the oven. Transfer to plate carefully.

Add 1 tablespoon of olive oil to the skillet. Add the mushrooms and cook until golden brown, approximately 8 minutes. Add onions and a sprinkle of salt and pepper. Continue to cook for 5 minutes or until the onions are softened.

Sprinkle flour and garlic powder over mushrooms and onions and stir. Add Marsala wine and bring to a simmer. Cook for 2-3 minutes until Marsala wine reduces slightly. Add chicken broth and chicken to the pan. Bring to a simmer. Then reduce heat to medium-low, cover, and cook for about 30 minutes, until chicken is cooked through, to internal temperature of 165 degrees F.

Once chicken is done cooking, transfer chicken thighs to a cutting board and shred the chicken. Return chicken to the skillet. Serve chicken marsala over a bed of pasta.

Notes

Growing up, my mom's Chicken Marsala was my favorite meal. Even through college I can remember asking her to make Chicken Marsala whenever I would come home to visit. My mom and I created a version that does not contain dairy that tastes just as good, if not better!

Ingredients

6 boneless, skinless chicken thighs

salt and pepper

2 tablespoons olive oil, separated

1 pound sliced white mushrooms

1 medium onion, chopped

3 tablespoons flour

1 teaspoon garlic powder

1 cup dry Marsala wine

1 cup chicken broth

1 pound pasta (spiral or egg noodles)

Rotisserie Chicken Salad

Serves 4-6

Instructions

In a large bowl, add ingredients and mix together well. Chill for an hour in the refrigerator.

Note

I love Waldolf chicken salad. I eat this salad on a sandwich, with pita or just eat it with a fork! When I have my friends over for lunch, this is an easy dish to make for multiple guests. I suggest buying a whole rotisserie chicken already cooked, on the bone, and pull the meat off the bones. It is packed with flavor.

Ingredients

4 cups cooked lemon-pepper rotisserie chicken, diced

2 celery stalks, chopped

1 cup red grapes, halved

1 cup walnut pieces

1 cup mayo

½ teaspoon lemon juice

salt and pepper to taste

Fish with Tomatoes and Olives

Serves 2

Instructions

Place cut tomatoes, olives, and capers in a medium size bowl. Set aside. Pat and dry fish and sprinkle salt and pepper on both sides. In a frying pan, heat olive oil on medium heat. Add fish and cook about 3-5 minutes per side depending on the thickness of the fish. The fish should flake when you push down with a fork, and it should not be translucent. Remove fish onto a plate and keep warm. To the hot frying pan, add tomatoes, olives, and capers. Cook for about a minute, stirring together softly, trying not to squish the tomatoes. Add white wine and cook another 3-4 minutes to reduce the wine by half. Stir in the vegan butter and parsley and cook until butter melts. Spoon mixture over the fish and serve warm.

Ingredients

1 large beefsteak tomato, chopped (approximately 1 cup)

½ cup kalamala olives, pitted and rinsed, cut in half

2 tablespoons capers

2-3 pieces of white fish, such as cod or tilapia

salt and pepper

2 tablespoons olive oil

½ cup dry white wine

1 tablespoon vegan butter

2 tablespoons chopped fresh parsley

Slow Cooker Chicken Fajitas

Serves 4

Instructions

Place chicken in the slow cooker and top with onions. In a bowl, mix together Italian dressing, lemon juice, and lime juice, and pour over chicken and onions. Cover and cook in slow cooker for 4 hours on high or 6-8 hours on low, until internal temperature of chicken is 165 degrees F. In the last hour of cooking, add the peppers. Once fajitas are finished cooking, shred chicken in the slow cooker using two forks. Fork fajita mixture onto warm tortillas and roll up.

Ingredients

2 large boneless, skinless chicken breasts

1 yellow onion, sliced

1 cup Italian dressing

juice of ½ lemon (approximately 1 tablespoon)

juice of ½ lime (approximately 1 tablespoon)

3 peppers, seeded and sliced (suggestion: use 1 red, 1 yellow, and 1 orange)

4 10-inch flour tortillas

Spicy Sausage and Broccoli Pasta

Serves 4

Instructions

In a large pot, bring salted water to a boil then add pasta. Cook according to the pasta package's directions, until pasta is al dente, soft but firm to bite. Carefully reserve 1 cup of pasta water, then strain the pasta.

Meanwhile, in a large skillet, on medium heat, squeeze sausage out of filling (if in casing), breaking it up into pieces as it cooks. Cook until sausage bits are lightly crispy. Add frozen broccoli. Cover and cook until broccoli is soft and defrosted (about 5-10 minutes), stirring occasionally. Add pasta with ½ cup of pasta water to sausage and broccoli. Continue cooking on low, mixing continuously for a few minutes. If dish looks dry, add the other 1/2 cup of reserved pasta water. Add pepper to taste.

Notes

I love this meal because it is only three ingredients and is still so tasty!

Ingredients

1 pound spicy Italian sausage

1 pound frozen broccoli

1 pound orecchiette pasta

pepper

Shrimp Rolls

Serves 4-6

Instructions

Preheat oven to 400 degrees F.

Shrimp should be defrosted if frozen. Pat dry with clean towel or paper towels to remove excess water. Spread shrimp on baking sheet. Drizzle with olive oil and sprinkle with Old Bay seasoning. Bake for 8-10 minutes. Do not overcook shrimp; they should be soft and juicy, not tough or rubbery. Allow shrimp to cool completely.

In a bowl, mix mayonnaise, celery, lemon, and dill. Using the fine side of a grater, grate the garlic clove into the mayonnaise mixture. Mix together well. Salt and pepper to taste. Combine cold shrimp with mixture. Fill bread rolls with shrimp and sprinkle with chopped dill.

Notes

My mom came over and told me she had delicious shrimp rolls and she wanted to recreate them. So we got into the kitchen and tried a few different combinations to create our recipe! Let's just say, we gobbled these shrimp rolls down before we even sat at the table for dinner!

Ingredients

1 ½ pounds raw shrimp, peeled and deveined

olive oil for drizzling

Old Bay seasoning

½ cup mayonnaise

¼ cup celery, minced

1 tablespoon lemon

1 tablespoon dill, plus 1 tablespoon for garnish, chopped

½ clove garlic

salt and pepper

6 rolls or hot dog rolls

Salmon Cakes

Makes 10 cakes

Instructions

Preheat oven to 350 degrees F.

Place salmon, skin side down, on a sheet pan. Drizzle with olive oil, salt and pepper. Cook for 15- 20 minutes until just cooked. Check by taking a sharp knife to peek into the thickest part. If the salmon is beginning to flake, but still has a little translucency in the middle, it is done. Remove from the oven, cover with aluminum foil, allow to rest for 10 minutes, and then refrigerate.

Place 2 tablespoons of oil and 2 tablespoons of vegan butter in a sauté pan. Add the celery, peppers, capers, hot sauce, ½ teaspoon salt, ½ teaspoon pepper, and Old Bay seasoning. Cook 15-20 minutes until soft. Remove from heat, add parsley, and mix. Cool to room temperature.

Flake chilled salmon into a large bowl, discarding the skin. Add mayonnaise, mustard, bread crumbs, and eggs. Add vegetable mixture and mix well. Chill in refrigerator for 30 minutes.

After mixture is chilled, shape into 2 - 3 ounce cakes, makes 10. Heat remaining 2 tablespoons of vegan butter and 2 tablespoons olive oil in large sauté pan over medium heat. Add salmon cakes and fry to 3-4 minutes on each side until browned. Drain on paper towels. Enjoy warm!

Tarter sauce: In a small bowl mix together mayonnaise, dill relish, lemon juice, and sprinkle of salt.

Notes

Enjoy the cakes dipped in homemade tarter sauce or on a bun with lettuce and tomato.

Ingredients

¾ pound salmon

olive oil

salt and pepper

4 tablespoons vegan butter, separated

3 stalks celery, finely chopped

1 yellow pepper, seeded and finely chopped

1 red pepper, seeded and finely chopped

1 tablespoon capers

¼ teaspoon hot sauce

½ teaspoon salt

½ teaspoon pepper

1 ½ teaspoons old bay seasoning

¼ cup parsley

½ cup mayonnaise

2 teaspoons mustard

1 cup plain bread crumbs

2 large eggs, beaten

Tarter Sauce Ingredients

½ cup mayonnaise

¼ cup dill relish

½ teaspoon lemon juice

sprinkle of salt

Kielbasa with Potatoes, Bacon, and Pineapple

Serves 6

Instructions

In a microwave safe dish, place potatoes and water. Cover and cook in the microwave until potatoes are tender, about 5 minutes. Drain water carefully. In a small bowl, combine brown sugar, vinegar, mustard, thyme, and pepper. Set aside.

In a large frying pan, on medium heat, add bacon. Cook until crispy, approximately 10 minutes. Carefully transfer bacon to cutting board and chop into pieces. Set aside.

To the large frying pan, heat the oil on medium heat. Add onion and kielbasa. Cook until onions are translucent, about 5 minutes. Add cooked potatoes and sugar mixture from the small bowl. Fry for another 5 minutes to allow the potatoes to crisp. Mix in bacon and pineapple, warm through, and serve.

Ingredients

1 pound medium sized red potatoes (about 3-4), washed and cut into ½ inch pieces

3 tablespoon water

2 tablespoons brown sugar

2 tablespoons cider vinegar

1 tablespoon mustard

½ teaspoon dried thyme

¼ teaspoon pepper

5 strips bacon

1 tablespoon olive oil

1 cup yellow onion, chopped

1 package Polish Kielbasa rope, cut into ½ inch slices

1 cup pineapple tidbits, drained (canned or use fresh pineapple and cut into small pieces)

Apple Cider Pork Chops

Serves 4

Instructions

In a skillet, heat oil on medium-high heat. Brown pork chops on both sides, approximately 3 minutes per side. Stir in chicken broth, soy sauce, and vinegar; bring to a boil. Reduce heat, cover and simmer until pork chops are tender and cooked through, 10-20 minutes depending on the thickness of your pork or until internal temperature 145 degrees F.

While the pork chops are cooking, in a small bowl, combine apple juice, brown sugar, and cornstarch, and stir until smooth. Remove chops from skillet and cover with foil. Increase heat to medium. Add apple juice mixture to skillet. Cook until thickened, stirring frequently. Add chopped apple and heat through. Spoon sauce over pork chops. I suggest serving with rice.

Ingredients

1 tablespoon oil

4 pork chops

1 cup chicken broth

2 tablespoons soy sauce

1 tablespoon apple cider vinegar

½ cup apple juice

2 tablespoons brown sugar

2 tablespoons cornstarch

1 large apple, peeled and coarsely chopped

Chicken Primavera

Serves 4-6

Instructions

Salt and pepper the chicken. Add flour to a large bowl and coat chicken in the flour. In a high sided sauté pan, heat oil on medium heat. Place chicken in pan and fry about 5 minutes per side until you get a nice crust. Remove chicken and place on a plate. Chicken will finish cooking later. In the same pan, sauté onions, peppers, and garlic for about 8-10 minutes until softened. Add wine and cook for about one minute, stirring and scraping the pieces off the bottom. Add tomato sauce, chicken broth, and capers. Stir all together. Return chicken to the pan and simmer for about 20 minutes, until chicken is cooked through, to internal temperature of 165 degrees F.

Salt and pepper to taste. Serve with pasta if desired.

Ingredients

4-6 chicken breasts or boneless thighs

salt and pepper

2 cups flour

2 tablespoons olive oil

1 yellow onion, sliced

2 green peppers, seeded and sliced

2 cloves garlic, minced

½ cup white wine

1 can (14 ounces) tomato sauce

1 can (14 ounces) chicken broth

2 tablespoons capers

Grilled Chicken with Cornell Marinade

Serves 4-8

Instructions

In a mixing bowl, beat the egg. Add oil and beat further. Stir in the cider vinegar, salt, poultry seasoning, and pepper. Place chicken in large containers with lids or gallon size zipper-top plastic bags. Pour marinade over chicken. Marinate chicken for 1 –2 days in the refrigerator. Grill chicken until cooked through, or until internal temperature is 165 degrees F. Usually takes up to an hour for chicken halves.

Notes

I love chicken BBQ! The smell of these salty tangy chickens cooking on the grill always reminds me of summertime.

Ingredients

1 egg

1 cup vegetable oil

2 cups cider vinegar

2 tablespoon salt

1 tablespoon poultry seasoning

½ teaspoon pepper

4-8 chicken halves

Sweet Chili Eggplant on Garlic Hummus Toast

Serves 4

Instructions

Preheat oven to 400 degrees F.

Slice eggplants to ¼ inch pieces, (cut off and discard the top and bottom slices of the eggplant). Place sliced eggplant on baking sheet lined with parchment paper. Spread a layer of sweet chili spread over eggplant. Bake for 30 minutes.

Toast the sliced bread. Spread garlic hummus over the toast and then place a slice of the cooked eggplant on the hummus. Repeat for each slice of toast.

Ingredients

2 eggplants

1 jar of sweet chili sauce

8 slices whole grain bread

1 container (8 ounces) garlic hummus

Fish Tacos

Serves 4

Instructions

Broccoli Slaw Directions

In a small bowl, mix vinegar, lime juice, honey, salt and pepper, olive oil, and cilantro. Add broccoli slaw and mix well together. Cover and refrigerate while cooking the fish.

Fish Directions

In a shallow bowl, mix bread crumbs and Old Bay seasoning. In a large skillet, heat oil over medium-heat. Dredge fish filets into bread crumb mixture, pat bread crumbs onto fish well, and then place the fish on the skillet. Cook for about 2 minutes per side until fish is cooked through and has a nice brown crust. Place cooked fish on a plate with a paper towel. Continue cooking fish in batches.

Ingredients

Broccoli Slaw Ingredients

¼ cup cider or white vinegar

1 teaspoon lime juice

2 tablespoons honey

salt and pepper

dash of olive oil

2 tablespoons cilantro, chopped

2 cups shredded broccoli slaw

Fish Ingredients

1 cup unseasoned bread crumbs

2 tablespoons Old Bay seasoning (can substitute Cajun or creole seasoning)

¼ cup vegetable oil

1 pound lake trout, cut into 2 inch filets, patted dry with paper towel

Fish Tacos Continued

Instructions

Tarter Sauce Directions

Mix together all ingredients in a small bowl.

Assemble Tacos

Lay out a small soft tortilla and spread a layer of tarter sauce on it. Then place a few pieces of fish and top off with broccoli slaw. Sprinkle with more cilantro if desired. Enjoy!

Notes

When I created this recipe, my dad had brought me fresh lake trout that he caught that morning. Any white mild fish, such as, flounder, halibut, cod, or shrimp would taste great with this recipe.

Ingredients

Tarter Sauce Ingredients

¼ cup mayonnaise

¼ dill relish

½ teaspoon lemon juice

salt and pepper

(Want to kick it up a bit? Add a few dashes of hot sauce to your tarter sauce!)

Seafood Fra Diavolo

Serves 4-6

Instructions

Cook pasta according to package. When complete, before draining, reserve ½ cup cooked pasta water. While pasta is cooking, in a large high-walled pan, on medium-high, heat one tablespoon of olive oil. On a separate plate, season scallops and shrimp with salt and pepper. In batches, add the scallops and shrimp to the pan and cook until just cooked (about 2 minutes per side). Transfer scallops and shrimp to a bowl and cover with foil to keep warm.

Add another tablespoon of olive oil to the pan if dry, then add garlic, shallots, crushed red pepper, and oregano. Continue to cook on medium-high heat until you can smell the garlic and it is softened (about one minute). Add tomatoes and bring to a boil. Bring heat to a medium and simmer for 5 minutes. Add the wine and cook for 5 more minutes. Stir in the pepperoncini peppers, brine, 1 tablespoon of parsley, and basil. Add the cooked scallops and shrimp. Stir well on low heat. Be careful around the scallops as you do not want them to break apart.

Add the bucatini pasta and ½ cup pasta water to the sauce. Mix the pasta into the sauce on low for 1-2 minutes until the sauce covers every noodle. Transfer to a bowl and top with fresh parsley for garnish.

Notes

If you want to add more seafood into your dish, consider adding little neck clams and crab. I would steam about 12-15 little neck clams until they open. Discard any that do not open. Remove meat from shell. Add the cooked clams and cooked lump crab meat when you add the cooked scallops and shrimp to the sauce.

Ingredients

10 ounces bucatini pasta

2 tablespoons olive oil, separated

¾ pound sea scallops

1 pound peeled and deveined large shrimp

salt and pepper

5 garlic cloves, minced

2 large shallots, finely shopped

½ teaspoon crushed red pepper

½ teaspoon dried oregano

1 can (28 ounces) whole peeled plum tomatoes, crush by hand

1 cup dry white wine

2 tablespoons pepperoncini peppers from the jar, plus 1 tablespoon brine from the jar

1 tablespoon parsley, plus 1 tablespoon for garnish, chopped

2 tablespoons basil, chopped

Additional Seafood Ingredients

12 little-neck clams

6 ounces cooked lump crab meat

Grilled Mushrooms

Serves 3-4

Ingredients

3-4 large whole portabella mushrooms

1 cup Italian dressing

½ cup sun-dried tomatoes, chopped

½ cup marinated artichokes, chopped

¼ cup capers, drained

Instructions

Take a wet paper towel and wipe any dirt off the mushrooms. In a gallon size zipper-top plastic bag, place mushrooms and coat with Italian dressing. Marinate for 15-30 minutes.

Place mushrooms out on a plate, bottom side up. Top with the sundried tomatoes, marinated artichokes, and capers. Add more if desired. Carefully transfer to the grill. Grill for 20-30 minutes. Serve warm.

Clam Bake Packets

Serves 4

Instructions

Cut aluminum foil into 2 feet long strips, two pieces per packet. Cross the foil pieces and make into the shape of a bowl. First drizzle olive oil onto the foil, approximately 1 tablespoon. In each packet, add potatoes, kielbasa, and a sprinkle of Old Bay. Then add shrimp and clams. Place corn on top. Sprinkle Old Bay seasoning, moderately. Add 2 tablespoons of vegan butter to each packet.

Bring up two sides of foil and seal the edges, making a tight 1/2-inch fold and fold again. Allow space for heat circulation. Fold other sides to seal. Place on the grill on medium flame for 20-30 minutes. Check a packet by carefully opening and see if the clams are open.

Spread olive oil on a loaf of bread and grill for 3-5 minutes, or until you have a slight char to the bread. Slice and serve on the side of clam packets to dip into the juices.

Notes

A clam bake makes me think of a hot summer day with friends and family hanging out, drinking a cold beer and enjoying buttery littleneck clams. Before we used the grill, clam bakes became a big production in the kitchen. We would cook corn, seafood, and salt potatoes inside. Who wants to be in the kitchen cooking when it's beautiful outside? We came up with a foil packet that contains all the food in one! Everyone gets their own packet to enjoy. You will not spend your evening cooking in the kitchen or cleaning up!

Ingredients

olive oil for drizzling

4 medium red potatoes cut in ¼ inch slice (one potato per packet)

1 pound package of kielbasa cut into ½ inch slices (about 6-8 pieces per packet)

Old Bay seasoning

1 pound uncooked tail-on shrimp, defrosted (approximately 6 per package)

40 fresh littleneck Clams (10 per package)

4 medium ears of sweet corn (1 per packet) cut into thirds

1 stick vegan butter, cut into tablespoon pieces

loaf of bread (optional)

Dessert

Chocolate Chip Cookies

Makes 2 dozen cookies

Instructions

Preheat oven to 375 degrees F.

In a small bowl, stir together flour, baking soda, and salt. Set aside. In a mixing bowl or using an electric mixer, add egg, vanilla, butter, brown sugar, and granulated sugar. Turn mixer on and set at medium speed until mixed, about 30 seconds. Stop to scrape the sides of the bowl. On low speed, add dry ingredients slowly until mixed well. Stir in the chocolate chips and oatmeal if desired. Line two baking sheets with parchment paper. Using a small spoon, drop rounded dough balls 2 inches apart onto baking sheets. Bake for 10-12 minutes. Let cool on baking sheets for 3 minutes. Then transfer to plate or wire rack.

Notes

The way to make chocolate chips cookies is to use dairy-free chocolate chips. This means searching your local grocery store and looking at the ingredients list to find dairy-free chocolate chips. You can eat cocoa butter but not milk containing ingredients: milk-chocolate, milk-fat, butter.

Ingredients

1 cup all-purpose flour

½ teaspoon baking soda

½ teaspoon salt

1 egg

1 teaspoon vanilla extract

½ cup (1 stick) vegan butter melted or at room temperature

½ cup light brown sugar

½ cup granulated sugar

1 cup dairy-free chocolate chips

½ cup oatmeal (optional)

Maple Coconut Cookies

Makes 4 dozen cookies

Instructions

Preheat oven to 375 degrees F.

In a bowl, whip the vegan butter and brown sugar. Mix in the egg, syrup, and vanilla until mixed well. In a separate bowl, mix flour, baking powder, and salt. Add dry ingredient mixture to wet mixture. Stir in the coconut. Using a tablespoon, drop balls of dough onto greased baking sheet. Bake for 12-15 minutes or until golden brown.

Ingredients

½ cup (1 stick) vegan butter, softened

1 cup brown sugar

1 egg

½ cup maple syrup

½ teaspoon vanilla extract

1 ½ cups flour

2 teaspoons baking powder

½ teaspoon salt

1 cup flaked coconut

Wacky Chocolate Cake

Serves 6-8

Instructions

Preheat oven to 350 degrees F.

Mix all ingredients together. Bake for 30 minutes in two 9 inch round cake pans or one 13x9 cake pan. When using cake pans, line with parchment paper inserts. Once cake has cooled, removed from cake pan onto serving platter. Sprinkle with powdered sugar if desired.

Ingredients

2 cups sugar

3 cups flour

⅔ cup cocoa

2 teaspoons baking soda

1 teaspoon salt

2 teaspoons vinegar

⅔ cup vegetable oil

2 cups water

1 cup non-dairy chocolate chips

powdered sugar (optional)

Carrot Cake

Serves 8-10

Instructions

Preheat oven to 350 degrees F.

In a small bowl, sift flour, baking powder, baking soda, salt, and spices. Set aside. In a medium sized bowl, mix together drained pineapple, grated carrots, and walnuts. Set aside. Using an electric mixer, on medium speed, mix sugar, vegetable oil, and vanilla. Scrape the sides of the bowl and mix until completely blended. Add the eggs one at a time, allowing to blend for 10 seconds after each egg and scraping the bowl after each egg. Add the dry ingredients and beat on low for 10 seconds. Then mix the batter with a spatula until the dry ingredients are incorporated. Add the pineapple mixture on low speed and mix for about 10 seconds.

Pour the batter into a well-greased Bundt pan. Bake in the center rack for 45 minutes. Cool in the pan for 20 minutes, then invert cake onto a wire rack and cool completely before frosting.

Notes

This cake recipe is so flavorful you really do not have to frost it! If I am serving carrot cake in the morning (with an nice hot cup of coffee or tea), I leave it unfrosted. If I am serving it in the evening as a dessert, I frost it!

Ingredients

2 cups all-purpose flour

2 teaspoons baking powder

1 ½ teaspoons baking soda

1 teaspoon salt

2 teaspoons ground cinnamon

½ teaspoon ground cloves

½ teaspoon ground allspice

1 cup crushed pineapple, drained

2 cups grated carrots (about 5 carrots)

½ cup chopped walnuts

1 ¾ cups sugar

1 ½ cups vegetable oil

1 teaspoon vanilla extract

4 eggs

dairy-free cream cheese frosting, recipe on page 101

Cream Cheese Frosting

Ingredients

½ cup (1 stick) vegan butter, room temperature

4 ounces dairy-free cream cheese

2 cups powdered sugar

1 teaspoon vanilla extract

Instructions

In an electric mixture, combine vegan butter and dairy-free cream cheese. Beat on medium-high speed until creamy. Slowly add 1 cup of powdered sugar, on low speed. Mix until combined, and then add the second cup. Add vanilla and increase speed to medium. Mix until smooth. Spread on the carrot cake (page 100).

Chocolate Covered Bananas with Peanut Butter

Ingredients

2-3 bananas, sliced into 1/2 inch pieces

¼ cup peanut butter

1 cup dairy-free chocolate chips

sprinkles

Instructions

Prepare a plate with parchment paper. Take your sliced banana and with a knife, place a small amount of peanut butter on each piece. In a microwave safe bowl, melt chocolate chips in the microwave; in 15 second increments, taking the bowl of chocolate out to stir each time until melted. Drop one slice of peanut butter banana at a time into the bowl. Using a spoon, dowse the chocolate over the banana. Place the chocolate covered banana on parchment paper and drizzle sprinkles over them while the chocolate is still warm. Repeat with all of your banana slices. Place in the freezer for at least an hour.

Notes

We visit the ice cream store often during the summer. I usually sit there while everyone enjoys their ice cream. When I saw a little girl eating a chocolate covered banana, I struck up a conversation with her mom. Her mom mentioned that her daughter could not tolerate dairy and the chocolate covered banana was vegan! This was a game changer for our ice cream visits! Let's just say every time we went, I would order three chocolate covered bananas to go and put them in my freezer for a nightly dessert, until I started making them from home!

Apple Crisp

Serves 6-8

Instructions

Preheat oven to 350 degrees F. Prepare an 8 inch glass baking dish with non-dairy cooking spray.

In a large bowl, mix together the apples, sugar, lemon juice, vanilla, cinnamon, nutmeg, and salt. Spread into prepared an 8 inch square glass baking dish.

In a medium bowl, add brown sugar and salt. Mix in the vegan butter until the mixture is wet. Add the flour and oats and stir until just mixed together. Spoon over apple filling.

Put the baking dish on a baking sheet and bake for 50-60 minutes. Bake until the filling is bubbling and the topping is golden brown.

Ingredients

2 Granny Smith apples, peeled and cut into 1 inch pieces

3 sweet apples (such as Empire, Red Delicious, Gala, Fuji, Honeycrisp) peeled and cut into 1 inch pieces

½ cup sugar

2 teaspoons lemon juice

1 teaspoon vanilla extract

1 ½ teaspoons ground cinnamon

½ teaspoon ground nutmeg

¼ teaspoon salt

1 cup firmly packed light brown sugar

¼ teaspoon salt

½ cup (1 stick) vegan butter, melted

1 cup flour

⅓ cup rolled oats

Index

A
Apple Cider Pork Chops, 81

Apple Crisp, 105

B
Baked Beans, 39

Baked Pancakes with Fruit Topping, 23

Banana Bread, 13

BBQ Chicken Pizza, 33

Beef Stew, 51

C
Carrot Cake, 100

Cauliflower Pizza Crust with Pesto, Tomatoes, and Artichokes, 31

Chicken Artichoke Soup with Quinoa, 55

Chicken Marsala, 65

Chicken Primavera, 82

Chocolate Chip Cookies, 95

Chocolate Covered Bananas with Peanut Butter, 103

Clam Bake Packets, 93

Corned Beef Sweet Potato Hash, 25

Cream Cheese Frosting, 101

E
Escarole and Beans with Sausage, 53

F
Fish Tacos, 87-88

Fish with Tomatoes and Olives, 69

Fruit Salsa, 37

G
Grandma Betty's Stuffing, 43

Grandma Irene's Manhattan Clam Chowder Soup, 57

Grilled Chicken with Cornell Marinade, 83

Grilled Mushrooms, 91

H
Hummus, 38

I
Italian Wedding Soup, 56

K
Kielbasa with Potatoes, Bacon, and Pineapple, 79

L
Lindsay's Chicken, 59

M
Maple Coconut Cookies, 97

Meatballs, 62

Meatloaf Muffins, 63

Mediterranean Zucchini, 41

Index

O
Oatmeal, 19

P
Pizza with Smoked Chicken Sausage, Brussels Sprout, and Honey Sweet Potatoes, 29

Potato Leak Soup, 49

Potato Salad, 35

Prosciutto Arugula Pizza, 27

R
Reney's Tomato Salsa, 46

Reuben Sandwich, 61

Rotisserie Chicken Salad, 67

S
Salmon Cakes, 77

Seafood Fra Diavolo, 89

Shrimp Rolls, 75

Slow Cooker Chicken Fajitas, 71

Spicy Sausage and Broccoli Pasta, 73

Strawberry Banana Smoothie, 22

Sweet Chili Eggplant on Garlic Hummus Toast, 85

T
Toast with Avocado and Eggs, 16

Toast with Peanut Butter and Banana, 17

V
Vanilla Chia Seed Pudding, 15

Vegetable Pesto Pasta Salad, 45

W
Wacky Chocolate Cake, 99

Y
Yogurt Parfait, 21

Made in United States
Orlando, FL
05 October 2023

37610706R00060